G

ANIMAL VISION

BY THE SAME AUTHOR

ANIMAL
VISION

written and illustrated by

GEORGE F. MASON

William Morrow and Company   New York

CONTENTS

INTRODUCTION

Long ago, when I first began to notice how animal eyes differ from human eyes, I used to wonder how certain animals could see in the dark while I couldn't see anything without the aid of artificial light. Other questions also began to occur to me. When a beam of light is focused on a cat's head at night, what makes the eyes shine so brightly? Why doesn't the same thing happen when a light is flashed toward my eyes at night? How can hawks and vultures, circling high in the sky, spot small prey or animal carcasses on the ground far below? How can a robin see ahead to capture a worm when the robin's eyes are on the side of its head?

Later, on hunting trips, I discovered that approaching wild game without being seen is far from easy. Do these animals have eyes that see in all directions at once? When skinning a grizzly bear, I noticed that the huge bear's eye is no bigger than a fox's eye. Does its little eye mean that its field of vision is small?

Another interesting observation aroused my curiosity. If an earthworm has no true eyes, why does the worm duck back into its burrow when a beam of light is flashed toward it at night?

After a good deal of research I have found the answers to most of these questions that perplexed me in the past. This book is written for the benefit of young naturalists who may be equally curious about animal vision and wish to learn how an eye is built and how various kinds of eyes solve the visual problems of animals inhabiting different environments.

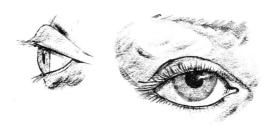

THE HUMAN EYE

To understand animal eyes, one needs to be familiar with the structure of the human eye and have some knowledge of the function of its chief parts.

First of all, the human eye sets in a bony socket. The delicate membranes of the exposed surface are protected by lids and eyelashes. The eyeball itself is quite round and firm. Its tough outer wall is a fibrous tunic firmly distended by pressure from fluids secreted in the front, or anterior, and rear, or posterior, chambers of the eye. The clear fluid in the front chamber is called the aqueous humor. In the back chamber, which is larger, the gelatinous, semisolid fluid is called the vitreous humor. The eye needs to be well protected from injury, because a wound puncturing the wall would release the pressure of the inner fluids and collapse the eyeball.

Now refer to the diagram showing a cross section of the human eye and note its general anatomy. Is it not built like a camera? Let us compare certain parts of the camera and eye to see how closely they function alike. The shutter of the camera and the eyelids both can be closed to exclude light. The camera lens is made up of two elements, front and rear, and they focus light onto a film. In the same way, human eyes have two lenses: the corneal, or outer, lens, which is the transparent outer surface of the eye, and the crystalline, or inner, lens, which is located inside the eyeball. Together they focus light upon the retina, which lies against the inner wall of the eye.

The camera has a diaphragm that can be adjusted to change the size of the opening through which light passes on its way into the camera. The performance of this device is duplicated in the eye by the iris, the colored area in back of the cornea. Usually the iris is brown or blue, but sometimes we see green, hazel, and other color variations among human beings. It adjusts the

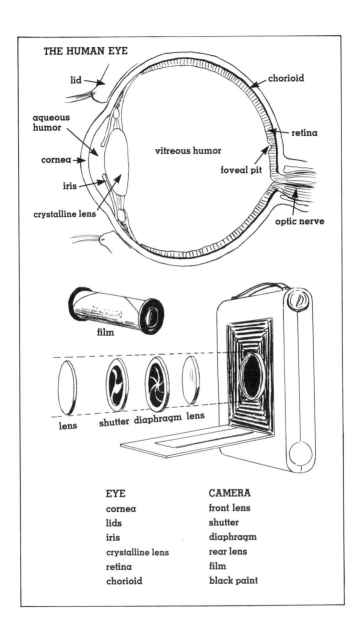

THE HUMAN EYE

lid

chorioid

aqueous humor

retina

vitreous humor

cornea

foveal pit

iris

crystalline lens

optic nerve

film

lens shutter diaphragm lens

EYE	CAMERA
cornea	front lens
lids	shutter
iris	diaphragm
crystalline lens	rear lens
retina	film
chorioid	black paint

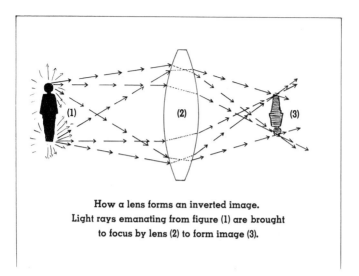

How a lens forms an inverted image.
Light rays emanating from figure (1) are brought
to focus by lens (2) to form image (3).

size of the pupil, which is the round hole in the center of the iris.

The inside walls of a camera are always painted black to prevent light reflections that could blur the film. A dark pigment, called the chorioid coat, covers the inside wall of the eye and performs the same service by preventing light reflections from blurring the image on the retina.

The camera and the eye are built so nearly alike that I wonder whether an eye could be used as a miniature camera. If a small strip of film could be inserted across the retina in the eye without collapsing the eyeball, wouldn't the lens of the eye focus an image on the film? Perhaps not, but the idea is interesting to speculate about.

When light rays reflected from objects reach the eye, they pass first through the outer lens formed by the transparent cornea and the aqueous humor. This lens bends, or refracts, light rays in focus through the pupil in the iris. The iris muscles relax or contract to expand or contract the pupil and thus control the amount of light that is permitted to pass through the center of the crystalline, or inner, lens and into the back chamber of the eye. By looking in a mirror, you can observe the changing size of the pupil as it adjusts for bright or dim light. When a beam of bright light strikes the eye, the pupil contracts quickly to its smallest diameter to prevent dazzlement. Take away the bright light, pull down the shades to darken the room, and the pupil expands to let in as much light as possible. The changes in the shape and size of the pupil are the only noticeable movements in the adjustments that take place within the eye, and for this reason the iris is a very interesting part of the ocular apparatus.

The crystalline lens in the human eye is also adjustable. The front side of the lens changes shape to accommodate light rays reflected from nearby objects. When we read fine print or survey objects within twenty feet, we are using the crystalline lens. A ring of muscle, called the ciliary

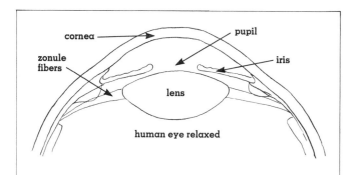

cornea

pupil

zonule
fibers

iris

lens

human eye relaxed

THE MECHANISM OF ACCOMMODATION

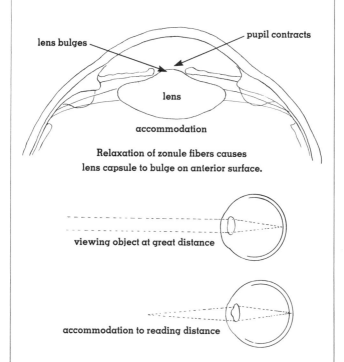

lens bulges

pupil contracts

lens

accommodation

**Relaxation of zonule fibers causes
lens capsule to bulge on anterior surface.**

viewing object at great distance

accommodation to reading distance

muscle, is attached to the lens by numerous threadlike fibers. Contraction of the muscle releases the pull on the fibers along the edge of the lens, causing it to change shape as its own elasticity draws it together. These slight movements bring close objects into focus on the retina.

Accommodation is a medical term used to describe the adjustments that move the crystalline lens either forward or backward or that change its curvature by squeezing or relaxing tension on it.

THE ANIMAL EYE

What does the world look like in the eyes of animals? Do a cat and a dog have the same visual image of their master? Many animals recognize people by scent. Are they also capable of distinguishing people and objects by sight? If so, different kinds of animals may have totally different visual impressions of the same person or object. There is no way of knowing what that mental picture is like, for the eyes of animals are extremely diversified and specialized structurally as the result of adaptation to different environments and living habits. Consequently each species may have a different visual impression of its surroundings.

Vision is a product of the eye and the brain.

The eye collects information, but the information does not become visible until after it travels along the optic nerve and enters the brain. Therefore, we must remember that the information gathered in animal eyes is limited not only by the specialized structure of their eyes, but also by the way in which their central nervous systems interpret the information.

The earthworm is an example of an animal that reacts to light and darkness, yet it has no eyes and cannot possibly see the difference between light and darkness. Scientists have learned that this behavior is due to the presence of a series of photosensory cells in the earthworm's skin.

A number of reports have been published suggesting that fish and certain primitive aquatic animals may not see anything even though they have good eyes. The theory is that when the information in the eye reaches the central nervous system, it sets off reflexes directing the body movements for such activities as procuring food, mating, and avoiding enemies. At no time, however, is the animal conscious of any visible sensation of light, shade, or color.

Whether or not there is any true vision in the brain cells of these animals is certainly difficult to determine when no one can be sure exactly how the senses are interpreted by any brain except his own. Still, much is known about the structure of the animal eye and how it works in different species.

THE LIDS

Eyelids are useful to most animals in the same way that they are useful to man. They shut to exclude light totally when the animal is sleeping or squint to protect against excess light when the animal is awake. In addition, they clean and moisten the exposed part of the eye and are a protection from windblown particles, sharp objects, and dangerous blows. Some aquatic animals, however, do not have lids. Their eyes are moistened by the water they live in. Still, many kinds of fish have a lidlike apparatus, called an adipose lid, that closes from side to side instead of up and down.

The frog's eye, which bulges out prominently, has an upper and a lower eyelid. I remember studying the structure when I was a boy. Gently I pressed a twig against an upper lid, and the eye sank down into the frog's head. The eye soon returned to its normal position after the pressure of the twig was removed. Having such protruding eyes, the frog needs to retract them for pro-

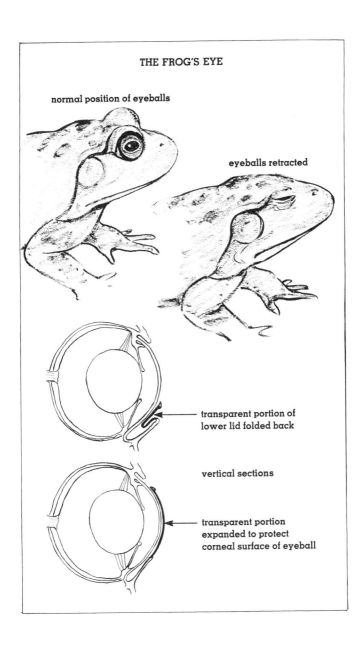

THE FROG'S EYE

normal position of eyeballs

eyeballs retracted

transparent portion of
lower lid folded back

vertical sections

transparent portion
expanded to protect
corneal surface of eyeball

tection when it burrows in mud or earth to hibernate for the winter. It can also raise its transparent lower lid across the eye.

This lid serves as a nictitans, a transparent membrane that can be moved across the eye at will. A nictitans is present in the eye structure of all birds and many mammals and amphibians. Among the birds, reptiles, and amphibians, this membrane is usually quite transparent and vision is not hampered while the nictitans covers the eye. Among the mammals, it is not transparent, but its movement is generally so rapid that it does not obstruct the animal's vision.

THE CORNEA

The transparent outer surface of the animal eye is called the cornea as is that of the human eye. It acts as a lens, and this corneal lens does most of the work of focusing the image onto the retina. Again the curvature of the cornea is maintained by pressure from the aqueous humor in the front chamber of the eye.

THE IRIS AND THE PUPIL

Often beautifully colored, bird irises can be black, brown, orange, red, green, gray, blue, or yellow, and there are variations of all these hues.

**cat's eyes adjusted
for dim light**   **cat's eyes adjusted
for bright light**

When dissecting the eye of an owl I was surprised to find the hinder surface of the bright yellow iris covered with a layer of dark pigment. It prevents reflections, which might blur the image on the retina, inside the eyeball as the chorioid coat prevents them in the human eye.

Most animals as well as human beings adjust the pupil size according to the amount of light they are exposed to, without any conscious effort. It is believed, however, that birds can control the iris at will. I have noticed the movements of the pupil in the eyes of parrots and chickens, and its size seemed to change continuously while the birds were looking at me.

Perhaps you are familiar with the peculiar ver-

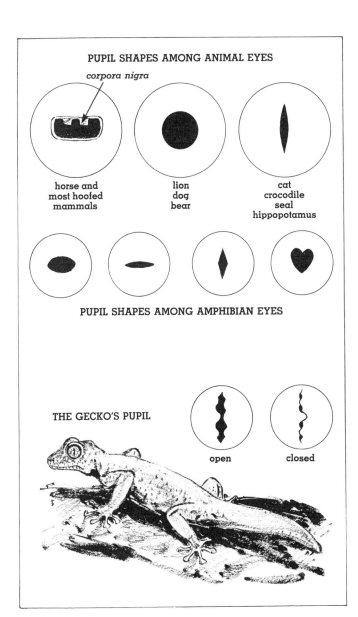

PUPIL SHAPES AMONG ANIMAL EYES

corpora nigra

horse and
most hoofed
mammals

lion
dog
bear

cat
crocodile
seal
hippopotamus

PUPIL SHAPES AMONG AMPHIBIAN EYES

THE GECKO'S PUPIL

open

closed

tical slit shape of a cat's pupil. You may have observed further that it is circular when fully dilated in dim light. Why the slit pupil? Domestic cats and several other kinds of animals, such as the foxes and the alligators, are active at night. These animals also like to bask in the sun during the daytime. This arrhythmic activity (no precise twenty-four-hour pattern of sleep and wakefulness) presents a problem in light control, which is solved partly by the slit pupil. It can dilate wide enough to gather sufficient light at night or contract narrowly enough to exclude the brilliant daylight that would dazzle the sensitive retina of a completely nocturnal animal.

The hoofed animals have horizontal pupils that tend to widen the field of vision beyond that attainable by round or vertical pupils. Some of these animals have developed peculiar devices for shielding the pupil from glaring light. The most curious are the fringelike curtains, called the *corpora nigra,* which are found along the pupil margins of horses, cattle, antelopes, camels, and various other hoofed animals.

Probably the greatest variety of pupil shapes occurs among the amphibians, some of which have oval, round, horizontal, diamond-shaped, heart-shaped, and rhomboidal pupils. All these pupils, however, are circular when they are dilated.

There is a most unusual pupil in the eye of a South American reptile called the gecko. The margins of the gecko's pupil have a number of notches that overlap when the pupil constricts. When the pupil is closed completely, the pattern of the notches leaves a vertical row of tiny pinholes through which light passes.

THE INNER LENS

The size and shape of the inner lens as well as its firmness or softness vary considerably in different kinds of eyes. If the shape is round or nearly round, the animal is able to see objects throughout a wide periphery without moving its head or eyeball. This structure is a great advantage, for it allows an animal to follow the movements of predators and hunters without making any motion revealing its location. Round lenses are typical among seals, fish, and small rodents.

Other lenses are biconvex. When they occur in this shape, the posterior side generally tends to be more convex than the anterior side.

The lens in a turtle's eye is the softest of any found among vertebrates. The turtle can change the shape of the lens easily by the action of

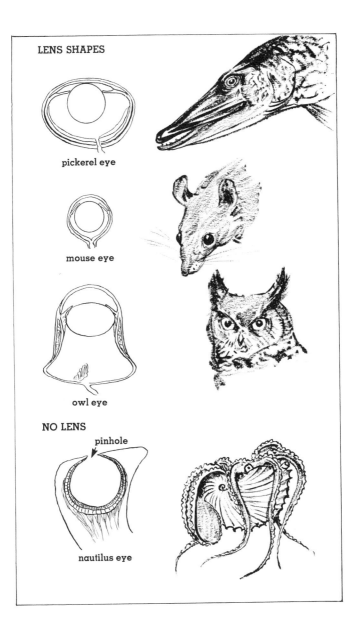

LENS SHAPES

pickerel eye

mouse eye

owl eye

NO LENS

pinhole

nautilus eye

sphincter muscles in the iris as well as those attached to the lens. This ability gives the turtle an enormous range of accommodation, either on land or in water, as it can regulate the curvature of the lens to focus on near or distant objects.

Other reptiles (except snakes) and amphibious birds have a similar muscular apparatus that changes the shape of the lens and adjusts vision either in water or air. Birds limited to aerial vision, however, do not depend upon the sphincter muscles of the iris to change the shape of the lens during accommodation.

The sharks, rays, snakes, and amphibians achieve accommodation by moving the lens forward toward the cornea. The lens of the bony fishes (telecosts) is drawn backward.

After boiling a codfish's head to make stock for a fish chowder, I found a perfectly round, white object in each eye of the fish. The boiling water changed the clear, inner lenses into hard, opaque balls that looked like white marbles. After drying out for a week, the white outer shell of both little balls cracked and peeled off, revealing a small translucent ball inside. These inner balls were about a quarter of an inch in diameter and, when held up to the light, appeared to be molded in sections like the inside of an orange.

Evidently the lens of a codfish's eye is composed of two different substances that solidify in boiling water.

Not all animals have an inner lens, however. The pinhole aperture in the eye of the chambered nautilus is one example of a substitute. It works like a pinhole camera, forming a sharp image on the retina without the use of any lens.

THE RETINA

The retina of the animal eye also lies against the inner wall of the eyeball. It is a transparent membrane in which there are millions of tiny nerve cells and other sensitive elements. The visual-cell layer stands on the external surface of the retina. There are two kinds of visual cells, called rods and cones, in this layer. The cones detect the lines, the points, and the colors of the image. The rods detect tones of light and dark, and distinguish outlines of objects in dim light.

The human retina has about twenty times more rods than cones. This proportion allows us to see colors and read fine print under good light conditions. We can see outlines and silhouettes of forms in dim light fairly well, but not as well as a cat or a flying squirrel, which have rod-rich retinas especially adapted for nocturnal vision.

The gray squirrel, being active only in the day-time, has a pure cone retina. As a general rule the retinas of nocturnal animals have more rods than cones, and diurnal (daytime) animals have more cones than rods. Animals, including the human being, having both rods and cones usually can adjust their vision for varying light conditions.

The horse's eyeball is shaped in such a way that the visual-cell layer is tilted; the upper part is progressively farther away from the lens than the lower part. By tilting the eye up or down, the horse places the image its eye transmits upon the visual cells at the proper distance from the

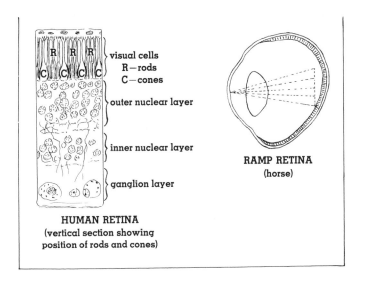

visual cells
R—rods
C—cones

outer nuclear layer

inner nuclear layer

ganglion layer

HUMAN RETINA
(vertical section showing
position of rods and cones)

RAMP RETINA
(horse)

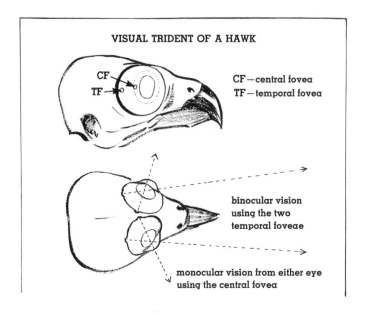

VISUAL TRIDENT OF A HAWK

CF — central fovea
TF — temporal fovea

binocular vision
using the two
temporal foveae

monocular vision from either eye
using the central fovea

lens in order to bring objects into focus over a considerable range of distance. This device makes accommodation by means of the inner lens unnecessary.

The flying fox, a large Australian fruit bat, has still another arrangement of the visual-cell layer. Its visual cells extend in a cone, from the retina, which places the cells at many different distances from the lens. Thus the animal is assured a sharp image of an object at any given distance, for the light rays always will be focused properly on some of the uneven layers of visual cells.

In eyes that are well adapted for daytime vision, there is a retinal area, containing a concentration of cones, that is called the *area centralis*. On this portion of the retina the image is sharper than on the rest of the retina. Some eyes also may have a fovea, which is a depression in the retinal tissue, in the *area centralis*. The sloping sides of the foveal depression reflect light rays in such a way as to magnify and thus sharpen the image when it reaches the visual-cell layer.

The fovea is well developed in the *area centralis* of birds such as the hawks, eagles, swallows, hummingbirds, and kingfishers, all of which have two foveae in each eye. The first, or central, fovea is used only for monocular vision when the bird is looking sideways. The second, or temporal, fovea works with the corresponding fovea in the other eye and is used for binocular vision when the bird is looking ahead.

Most domestic and ground-feeding birds have only one fovea in each eye.

EYE POSITION

As a rule, the eyes of predaceous animals are set in the front of the head and the eyes of their prey on the sides of the head. Birds of prey and the carnivorous mammals are more dependent upon a good view of the victims they pursue than they are upon hindsight, so having frontal vision is an advantage for them. The primates and a number of other more or less omnivorous animals also have frontally located eyes, but most defenseless small animals and the larger herbivores tend to have laterally located eyes. This position increases their field of vision in all directions.

Birds provide many interesting examples of specialized eye position. The bittern's eyes are set on the underside of its head. When a person

36

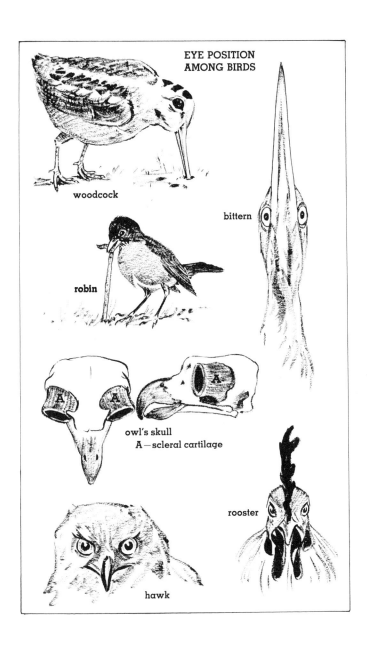

EYE POSITION
AMONG BIRDS

woodcock

bittern

robin

owl's skull
A—scleral cartilage

rooster

hawk

or dangerous animal approaches the vicinity of a bittern, the bird will often try to escape detection by standing motionless with its beak pointed straight upward. While in this position the bird is likely to be mistaken for a stick, because its long, pointed beak blends with the lines of the tall grass and reeds that are characteristic of its environment. Furthermore, the bird can follow the movements of an enemy while its head is in this awkward position, because its eyes are then directed forward and parallel to the ground.

The woodcock's eyes are near the top of the head, so that it can see its surroundings while its long beak is buried in the soft earth probing for worms.

I used to wonder how a robin sees to grasp a worm with its beak. The explanation is that the robin's beak is very narrow and in addition the eyes are set at a slight forward angle allowing the bird to have both binocular and monocular vision. That is, the robin can focus both eyes together in front of the beak and can focus each eye separately on either side of the beak.

The owl's eyes are set on the front of the head, so the owl has binocular vision directed forward. When skinning a great horned owl I noticed that the bird's eyes were set inside tubes that extend outward from the skull like a pair of binocular frames. I learned later that these tubes are cartilaginous cups which are surrounded by a series of bony plates called the scleral ossicles. Common to the eyes of all birds and most reptiles, the scleral ossicles play an important role in the mechanism of accommodation. They stiffen the wall of the eye against the pressure that is created whenever the inner lens moves forward.

The owl is probably the only bird that can fly in total darkness and capture its prey. The barn owl's extraordinary hearing sense is so keen that it can locate a mouse's position up to twenty feet away in total darkness if the mouse makes any sound that reveals its presence. Perhaps the peculiar concave depression formed by the feathers around the owl's eyes helps to gather sound waves like the apparatus used for recording birdsongs.

Since human eyes are in the front, we have an understanding of the benefits and limitations of having eyes in this position. Not many of us realize, however, the extent of the visual field that is possible when eyes are laterally placed in the head. The rabbit's eyes bulge from the sides of its head, allowing the rabbit to see an owl swooping down from above or a fox coming from

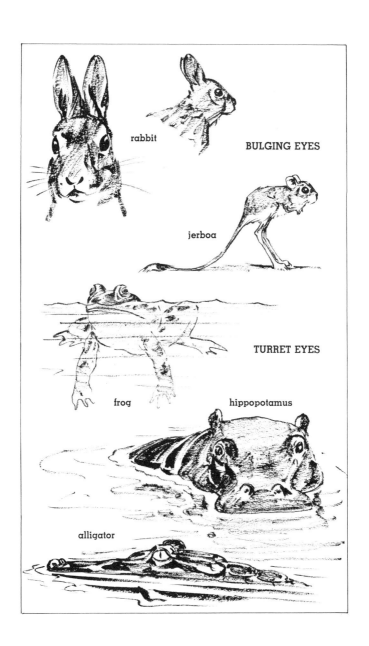

rabbit

BULGING EYES

jerboa

TURRET EYES

frog

hippopotamus

alligator

behind. At the same time, the rabbit sees ahead to avoid running into obstacles while fleeing from its enemy. The rabbit's extensive visual field is surpassed only by the jerboa, a small kangaroo-like rodent inhabiting North Africa and parts of Asia. Each of its laterally placed eyes sees more than a half circle, and together they see in every direction around the head.

We can detect movement out of the corner of our eye, which covers a visual angle of approximately 150 degrees. In comparison, the single eye of a domestic cat sees through an angle of 200 degrees; a horse sees through 215 degrees. Where the angles of vision are separate, there is monocular vision. Where the angles of vision overlap in front, behind, or above, there is binocular vision. Binocular vision enables animals to judge form and depth. When each eye is focused on the same object, the likeness of that object appears on the two retinas. Although the images are slightly different (due to the distance between the two eyes), they blend in the mind as a single picture having form and distance. We call this blending of two slightly different views stereoscopic vision.

The horse has almost complete periscopy (viewing all around). With its head up, it can see behind while facing forward. Using both

monocular and binocular vision, a horse is able
to see anything that moves in any direction while
holding its head in one position.

Such wide angles of vision enable animals to
remain motionless as they focus their eyes upon
the movements of predators. The rabbit does not
roll its eyes or move its head to follow the prog-
ress of a fox approaching its runway. The slightest motion of the rabbit's eye or head would liter-
ally be a dead giveaway. Many animals instinc-
tively avoid detection by freezing their position
and not blinking an eye.

The eye sockets of some animals protrude
above the head. We see this condition among
certain aquatic animals such as the alligator,
crocodile, hippopotamus, and some amphibians.
These animals are not strictly aquatic, since they
find most of their food on land or in the air.
Nevertheless, they all spend a lot of time swimming or floating in water, using their eyes like
periscopes while the head is submerged. As they
use their eyes primarily for aerial vision, their
aquatic vision is not good.

The chameleon has the most unusual example
of the protruding eye. This amazing lizard can
move its turretlike eyes separately in any direction and focus each eye on a different object.

COLOR VISION

The frequency and intensity of light emanating from objects and their surroundings arouses the sensation of color in the mind. Apparently no light or object in nature has any color. Instead the chemico-physical nature of the material observed reflects a certain wavelength. The longest visible wavelength is 760 millimicrons, and it arouses the sensation of red in the mind. But the eye sees the object rather than the light waves so the sensation of red is projected back to the object.

In any case, we know that the human eye sees color, but when it is said that an animal can or cannot see color, someone is sure to ask, "How do you know?" We don't know for certain, but through various experiments investigators have found evidence that some animals have color vision. Despite the most elaborate research procedures, however, the evidence is often difficult to interpret, for what appears to be the perception of color may be the recognition of form or brightness.

There are brilliant and beautiful colors on the wings of moths and butterflies, in bird plumage, and in the markings of reptiles, amphibians, mammals, and fish. Various invertebrates secrete colorful designs into their marvelous shells. Nevertheless, color has no esthetic value for animals. The possibility that a peahen admires the exotic colors of a peacock's spreading train is most unlikely. However, the peacock's colorful display attracts the hen's attention and arouses her mating instinct, so color does play an important role in controlling her instinctive behavior.

In a somewhat similar way, a man who drives a car automatically goes through the process of stopping the car when a red light flashes at an intersection. When the light turns green, he goes ahead. While obeying traffic signals is not exactly instinctive action, a man normally responds to these signals, due to long experience, without stopping to think over the mechanical details in-

COLORFUL LURES
THAT CATCH FISH

volved. In other words, the effect of the traffic lights on his vision makes him react to colors automatically.

During courtship activity among some birds, fish, and primates, the males often display their colors. Their coloring has no effect on the courtship behavior of any animal except their own species. When the male prairie chicken inflates its orange-colored air sacs, the mating instinct of the hen responds to the actions and colors of the male. But a female ruffed grouse would pay no attention to the most colorful and lively performance of a male prairie chicken. She can be won only by the somber colors and courtship activity displayed by a male ruffed grouse.

Anglers, particularly the dry-fly purists and plug fishermen, believe that the colors of their flies and plugs are very important. They have drawn the conclusion that trout and salmon have color vision, because they say that these fish strike at certain definite color patterns in preference to others.

Judging from the varieties of gaudy colored plugs and patterns of flies that are on the market, anglers think fish must be the most color-conscious animals in the world. While experiments have revealed that some fish show evidence of color vision, there is no proof that all fish have the same ability to see colors. Drawing upon my own experience, I have found that a black fly is as successful for catching a trout as any colorful pattern, and I am puzzled by the fact that bass strike at a plug at night when it is so dark I cannot see the surface of the water. Surely color is of no importance then, so the shape and action of a lure may be the attraction instead of color even in daylight. If the truth were known, colorful fish lures attract more anglers than fish.

Some time ago I had occasion to ask an ornithologist about the habits of the bower bird. Bower birds build structures with sticks and grass and decorate them with colorful collections of stones, shells, feathers, and other small objects. The ornithologist told me an interesting story about the satin bower bird of Australia. When it is between four and seven years old, the male bird's plumage turns from green to blue. Since he always selects *blue* objects when decorating his bower, he evidently is matching them with the color of his own plumage. He is particularly fond of blue feathers shed by other birds, blue flowers, and blue papers, crockery, and glass. Such evidence of color discrimination is proof that the satin bower bird has color vision.

SATIN BOWER BIRD

ANIMALS BELIEVED TO HAVE COLOR VISION

some insects

birds

turtles

most primates

some fish

What knowledge there is about color vision among animals has come from research on the structure of their visual cells and through experiments with animals in and out of laboratories. Although their opinions are not always in agreement, biologists in general believe that birds, lizards, turtles, most fish, some insects, and many of the primates (apes, baboons, chimpanzees, gorillas, and diurnal monkeys) can see and distinguish hues in the color spectrum. Furthermore, there is always the possibility that the eyes of some animals may be sensitive to light wavelengths that allow them to see colors which the human eye never sees.

In a group by themselves are the hoofed mammals, larger carnivores, rodents, and amphibians. All of these animals are believed to have no color vision or such a faint perception of color that they are practically colorblind.

Many of us are familiar with the popular notion that bulls are enraged at the sight of a red garment. Several experiments with male cattle revealed that the bull's attention is directed toward any unfamiliar, fluttering object no matter what its color may be. Red apparently has nothing to do with arousing the animal's emotions.

Deer hunters, obliged by law to wear bright

red garments when hunting, have discovered much to their surprise that their colored clothes do not make them any more conspicuous to the deer. These hoofed animals have no color vision, but their eyes detect the slightest motion of any familiar object. Most experienced hunters know that a deer seldom pays any attention to a motionless man, if it cannot catch his scent, no matter how much color he may have on his clothing.

I doubt that any country lad ever failed to use a scrap of red flannel or other red material on a fishhook when jigging for frogs. Red looks so bright to his eyes, he thinks it is highly effective as a lure. If he attached a small green leaf to the hook, however, he would discover that frogs show just as much interest in green as red. The action and not the color of the object on the hook is what interests the frogs. In fact, a frog would starve to death if the food around it remained motionless.

NIGHT VISION

No doubt you have envied the ability of some animals to see in the dark. What is the secret of night vision that enables them to lead a nocturnal existence?

First, you must understand that no animal can see when there is no light. If a cat and a man were placed inside a room with no doors or windows to admit light, both would be equally blinded. Out of doors, at night, however, there is enough light for nocturnal animals to see, because their eyes are adapted for night vision. Relatively larger than those of diurnal animals, their eyes have pupils that dilate enormously to take in as much light as possible. The retina is extremely sensitive and composed of masses of rods that detect faint light in the nighttime.

Several photochemical substances play a part in the light sensitive mechanisms of the retina. One called rhodopsin helps the eye to adjust for vision in the dark. The work of rhodopsin is noticeably effective in our own eyes when we pass from bright light into the dark.

Try out a simple experiment yourself by turning out all lights and standing in a darkened room. At first you will be unable to see any objects, but in a few minutes your eyes will adjust so that you can see the form of a chair or desk or whatever other furniture may be present. The adjustment of your eye to the dark interior is made possible by the formation of rhodopsin, which increases the sensitivity of the rods in your retinas.

Now switch on the bright lights. You immediately squint because the light dazzles your eyes, which are rendered supersensitive by the rhodopsin. But in a few minutes the rhodopsin bleaches out of the rods, and the eye is comfortably adjusted for bright light again. Rhodopsin is an active ingredient in the visual cells of all nocturnal vertebrate animals.

Eyeshine is another interesting feature of the

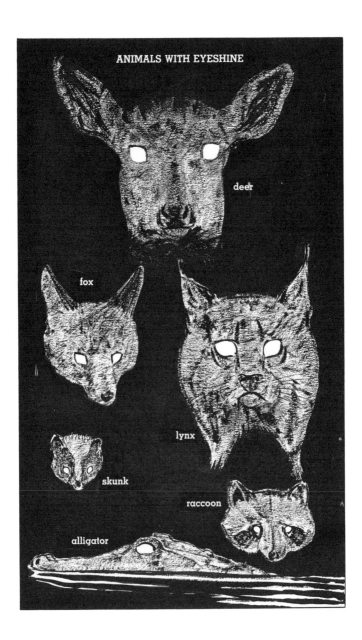

ANIMALS WITH EYESHINE

deer

fox

lynx

skunk

raccoon

alligator

owl

night hawk

BIRDS WITH GOOD NOCTURNAL VISION

whippoorwill

dark-adapted eye. The phenomenon of light reflecting from an animal's eyes at night can be seen when a beam of light from a flashlight or from car headlights reveals a pair of eyes shining brightly in the darkness. This peculiar eyeshine, more noticeable in the eyes of some animals than others, is caused by light reflecting from a mirror-like device called the *tapetum lucidum.* Usually the tapetum is located in the chorioid coat behind the visual cells. When a beam of light enters the eye, it passes through the visual cells and meets the tapetum, which reflects the light back through the visual cells and on out of the eye again. The natural function of eyeshine is to increase the intensity of dim light by reflecting it back through the visual cells.

The owls, nighthawks, whippoorwills, and woodcocks are active during the night, but most birds are diurnal and their eyes are not adapted for seeing in darkness. The flying squirrel, which is nocturnal, has eyes that are different from those of all the other members of the squirrel family. The structure of the flying squirrel's eye is right for night vision, but not as good for bright light. Chipmunks, red and gray squirrels, and all ground squirrels are diurnal animals, and their eyesight is limited strictly to daytime use.

I wonder if each animal's behavior has been influenced by the structure of its eye, or has the eye developed gradually to fit the animal's environment and living habits? We know that many animals change their habits over a span of time. Some diurnal animals, such as the beaver, have gradually switched from day to night activity. Over a period of time, they found night a better time to avoid the hunters and certain predatory animals. Did their eyes develop structural changes for nocturnal use gradually or were they always able to adjust to either bright or dim light?

The animals that are strictly nocturnal usually sleep in some darkened retreat during the day, but they may be routed out of their slumbers by a predator. While their eyes are uncomfortably dazzled in bright light, these animals are able to reduce the effect of the glare by squinting their eyelids over the contracted pupil.

Cattle, horses, deer, and all the carnivorous animals are able to see well enough in dim light to be active at night.

AQUATIC VISION

In addition to fishes, there are many mammals, birds, reptiles, amphibians, and invertebrates that have eyes especially adapted for underwater vision. A number of these animals are semiaquatic (even some fish); that is, they spend part of their life in water and part on land. Consequently, the eyes of such animals are often adapted for vision in both environments.

Let us first consider the fish's eyes. Usually they are placed laterally in the head, but there are many strange variations. The flounder's eye, for example, migrates over the top of the head, coming to rest beside the other eye on the upper side of the fish. Like the flounder, most fish that live on the bottom look upward.

Other fish are surface creatures. The turret-eyed mudskippers can raise and lower their eyes, so that they can see in all directions either in water or on land.

The four-eyed fish of South America, called Anableps, probably has the most remarkable eyes in the world. It is a top minnow that swims at the surface with its eyes half in and half out of the water. The Anableps' eye, therefore, is adapted for two kinds of vision. It has two pupils; the upper is used for aerial vision and the lower for aquatic vision. Inside there are two separate regions in the retina and a single pear-shaped lens. Such an elaborate optical system enables the fish to use the corneal surface as a lens for aerial vision above water while simultaneously focusing through the long axis of the inner lens onto another part of the retina for aquatic vision.

Submerged, the cornea ceases to be useful as a lens because the refractive power of its curved surface is lost when it is covered with water. That is, the lens can no longer bend parallel light rays and bring them to a focus.

Another curious adaptation occurs in the eye of the rock blenny, an amphibious fish that spends its time in the surf as well as on the rocks out of water. The blenny's eye appears to have

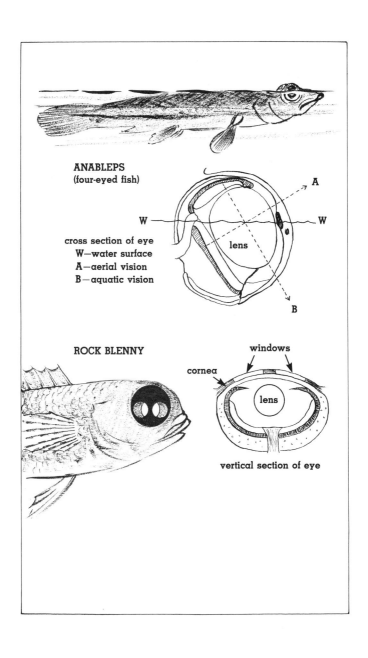

ANABLEPS
(four-eyed fish)

cross section of eye
W—water surface
A—aerial vision
B—aquatic vision

W

W

A

B

lens

ROCK BLENNY

windows

cornea

lens

vertical section of eye

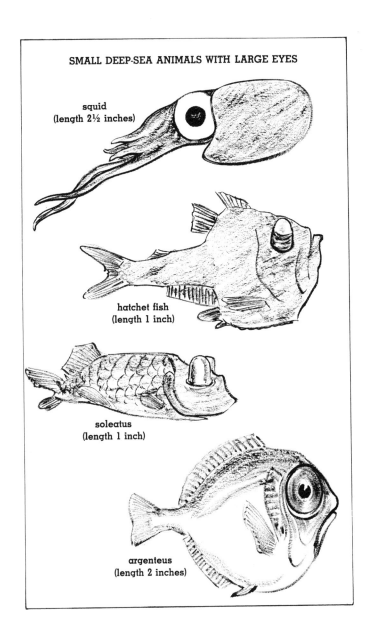

SMALL DEEP-SEA ANIMALS WITH LARGE EYES

squid
(length 2½ inches)

hatchet fish
(length 1 inch)

soleatus
(length 1 inch)

argenteus
(length 2 inches)

two pupils, but the pupillike openings are actually two separate clear areas in the cornea, which is otherwise darkly pigmented. The darkened cornea appears to be useful as an eyeshade when the fish is out of water, and the two clear areas allow sufficient light to pass through for aerial vision.

Although most naturalists and students are familiar with the story of the eel's life history, probably many of them may not be aware that at a certain stage its small eye grows rapidly to enormous size. This remarkable change in the growth of the eye takes place shortly before the adult eel leaves the inland ponds and streams to make the long journey to its breeding place somewhere in the Sargasso Sea near the West Indies. Within a few months' time the eye grows to a relatively large size and develops an increased sensitivity to light. By the time the eel reaches its destination in the darkened depths of the Sargasso Sea, its eyes are fully adapted for vision in a deep-sea environment.

Some cave-dwelling and deep-sea fishes are totally blind while others living in a lightless environment have retained large, well-developed eyes. Why would these fish have any use for vision at depths where there is no light? The answer is that there is light, a strange light created by light organs in the bodies of many deep-sea animals. Scientists have estimated that two thirds of all deep-sea fish species are luminous. There would be no purpose in fish producing light if there were no eyes to see it. In total darkness each luminous organism helps fish to locate food, avoid dangerous enemies, and distinguish their own kind.

Still, among all vertebrate animals, fish are best qualified to survive in a blind state because many of them locate food and detect vibrations by means of highly developed sensory nerve endings in their body. Very seldom can any of the other vertebrates survive without vision.

In the upper levels of water, sunlight penetrates to a depth of several feet, and in this area fish make good use of their eyes. With them, they distinguish their enemies and prey, and they can see through water and air at the same time, which is something the human eye cannot do.

The peculiarities of fish vision from water to air are such that when a fish looks in an upward direction it views the outside world through a circular window on the surface of the water. The diameter of the window is established by the distance from the fish's eyes to the surface. Since

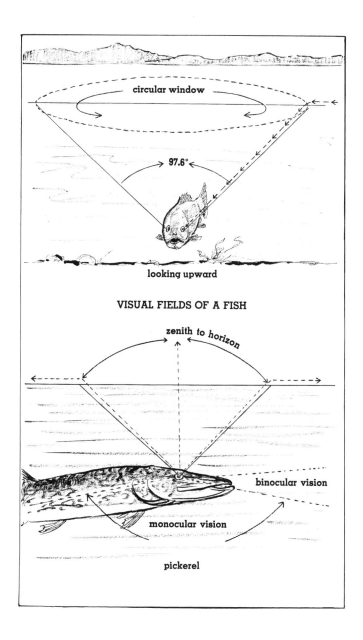

circular window

97.6°

looking upward

VISUAL FIELDS OF A FISH

zenith to horizon

binocular vision

monocular vision

pickerel

the angle of vision from the fish's eyes to the surface is always 97.6 degrees, the lower the position
of the fish, the greater the diameter of the window. When the water is shallow and calm, the
surface around this window acts like a mirror
and reflects the bottom of the pond.

If we did not know that light rays passing
through the rarer medium of air bend when they
enter the denser medium of water, we might sup-
pose that the fish's upward vision through the
surface window would be limited to a small portion of the sky directly over its head. But since
light rays from objects on the bank are refracted
downward in the water, the fish can see every-
thing from the zenith to the horizon, even though
its angle of vision upward is confined within the
perimeter of the window.

Swift-moving fish have streamlined, oval-
shaped eyeballs. Being covered at all times with
water, the cornea has no use as a lens. All focusing is done with the single inner lens. Accommodation is achieved by drawing back the round,
crystalline lens inside the eye. Among most of
these fishes, the eyeball bulges outward, allowing
good binocular vision forward, backward, and
upward as well as monocular vision on either side
of the head.

Several kinds of mammals spend a good part of their life in the water. Mink, otter, beaver, seal, sea lion, polar bear, and walrus capture their food or work under water. Not all of these animals have been studied to determine how well they can see when submerged, but I think they would have good aquatic vision in order to find their food.

The seal's eye is one that has been investigated, however, and the findings are quite interesting. It proved to be astigmatic due to an unusual refractive condition of the cornea. Astigmatism is caused by a defect in the shape of the corneal lens that prevents the rays from an object from being brought to a single focal point and thus produces blurring. Since the refractive power of a lens is lost in water, the condition of the cornea has no adverse effect on the seal's aquatic vision, which is very good because the eye is large and the pupil can expand widely. When the seal is out of water, its eye views the surroundings through a contracted slit pupil, which eliminates the astigmatism effectively. As a result, the seal sees well enough in the air to detect enemies over a hundred yards away.

Except for penguins, most amphibious birds probably have excellent aerial vision too. The

snakebird
(anhinga)

penguin

kingfisher

BIRDS WITH
UNDERWATER
VISION

water ouzel

birds that prey on small, fast-moving fish must see well underwater, or they would never be able to capture a darting fish. The cormorants, loons, grebes, auks, sheldrakes, and anhingas all feed on live fish, which they pursue underwater. The anhinga, perhaps better known as the Florida snakebird, does not catch a fish by grasping the victim in its bill as the other birds do. The snakebird spears its prey with its needle-sharp beak. Spearing small fish certainly requires good aquatic vision.

Among the small birds, the kingfisher and the water ouzel need to see underwater. The kingfisher perches on a branch over a body of water and keeps an eye focused down looking for a fish. When it spots one, the kingfisher dives through the air and grasps the fish, which may be swimming some distance below the surface.

The water ouzel, a small slate-colored songbird, lives along the rushing streams in the mountainous regions of the West. It has the remarkable ability to walk around on the bottom of the stream bed, even when the water is deep and fast. There it searches among the pebbles for its food, which consists of small aquatic insects. I often wonder how the bird overcomes the buoyancy that should be caused by the air spaces under its waterproof feathers.

Some amphibious birds have a protective device, which is comparable to a swimmer's face mask, for their eyes. It is a nictitating membrane, and it has a clear window, like a lens, in its center. The window is composed of a highly refractive substance that can bend light rays underwater.

INVERTEBRATE EYES

A good hand lens or, better still, a microscope is essential for studying the anatomy of small creatures like insects and spiders. Magnification reveals their remarkable features, which are practically invisible to the naked eye, and we find that some tiny insects look like prehistoric monsters when seen through the lens of a microscope. One can't help but feel that we are fortunate such fearful-looking animals never developed to be the size of elephants. The reason insects have never grown to be very large is that they breathe by means of tracheal tubules and that this respiratory system cannot supply enough oxygen for animals larger than a very small mouse.

Nearly all adult insects have eyes. Many have

two kinds—a pair of compound eyes and several small, simple eyes. The compound eyes are used for distant vision and the simple eyes for seeing objects nearby. Certain insects inhabiting darkened caves, however, are blind.

The large pair of eyes on either side of an insect's head are the compound eyes. Each one is composed of many tiny eyes packed closely together. When seen through a microscope, the little lenses appear to be symmetrically arranged in a mosaic pattern that covers the entire corneal surface of the eye. These little lenses are called corneal facets, and they vary in number among the different kinds of insects. A Brazilian species of beetle is said to have only seven of equal size, while the huge eye of a dragonfly has twenty thousand or more and the hawkmoth has twenty-seven thousand. The ant has fifty corneal facets, and an ordinary housefly has four thousand. The size of the facets also varies considerably in proportion to the size of the insect.

Compared with the eyes of vertebrate animals, the compound eyes are extremely complex and delicately organized. Each tiny facet (some of which are only one two thousandth of an inch in diameter) is composed of a lens behind which there is a cone, a rod, nerve fibrils, and the basal

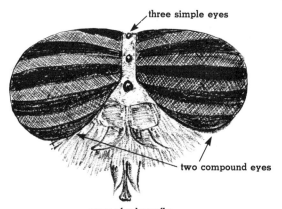

three simple eyes

two compound eyes

eyes of a horsefly

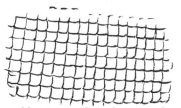

pattern of facets on surface of compound eye

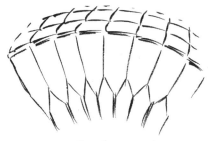

cross section of compound eye

THE FLY'S EYE

membrane, which perceives the image and transmits it to the brain. The cones and rods are surrounded by a pigment that prevents light rays from passing from one facet to another.

There is a good deal of speculation about the impression a compound eye transmits to the insect's brain. The most favored view among experts suggests that each facet in a compound eye transmits a separate image. If this theory is so, the compound eye visualizes a mosaic pattern of images instead of a single uninterrupted picture. Scientists also generally believe that many insects distinguish colors, including some that are invisible to the human eye.

Last summer I killed a number of horseflies gathered on the windshield of a parked car. Out of curiosity, I decided to see what they looked like under the lens of a microscope. Placing a fly on a glass slide, I focused the lens on the head and, much to my surprise, saw several brilliant blue, green, and red bands of color running across the fly's compound eyes. The colors faded out within a few hours.

Further examination of the area between the compound eyes revealed three black, shiny spots of different sizes. These spots are also eyes, but they are called simple eyes.

The simple eyes (ocelli) on an insect's head vary in number, three being the most common. Structurally, each eye is composed of a lens, cones, and nerve rods connected by nerve fibrils to the optic nerve. It is generally believed that these simple eyes see objects only a few inches away.

An issue of *Life* magazine recently printed a photograph taken through the three simple eyes of a dead wasp. This remarkable picture shows how each tiny lens focused on the body of another wasp poised a few inches above. While it illustrates the power of the lens and the field of vision in a simple eye, we cannot assume that the wasp has the same visual impression as that recorded on the camera film. We do not know how an insect's brain interprets visual information. This primitive brain may never see a mental image such as that which occurs in the conscious minds of more highly developed animals and man. For all we know, an insect's reflexes may respond to visual stimulation much as the mechanical movements of a robot respond to an electric eye.

Scientists continually are studying the vision of insects. They have even gone as far as to plant tiny electrodes in the optic nerve fibers behind a

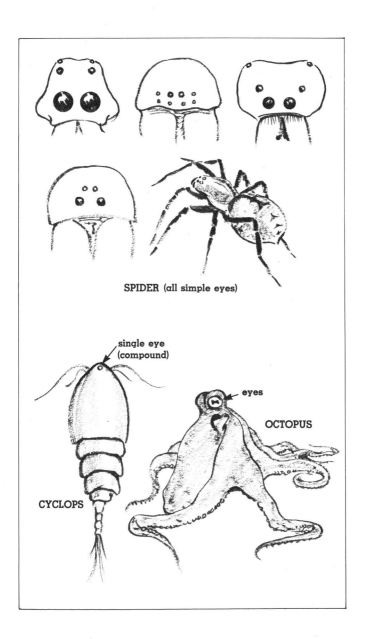

SPIDER (all simple eyes)

single eye
(compound)

CYCLOPS

eyes

OCTOPUS

fly's eye in an effort to determine the fly's reaction to visual stimuli. Through these experiments they learned that a fly's eye has about the same capability as the human eye for observing dim objects, and its light-gathering power about equals that of the human eye.

Spiders have simple eyes, but they do not have compound eyes. One can see easily the brightly polished lenses of the spider's eyes, for they are located usually on the front part of the head. They always remind me of the windows in front of the pilot on a big aircraft as they are symmetrically arranged in groups of eight, six, four, or two, depending upon the species. Among the various structures eight is the number most frequently observed. How far these simple eyes see objects clearly is difficult to determine, but their vision probably is quite good for short distances, judging from the way some spiders pounce on their prey. In fact, the Bolas spider sees well enough to capture a flying moth by throwing a sticky ball of silk at it.

In the realm of nature there is always something new to learn. I never realized that a horseshoe crab has two pairs of eyes until I read an article recently about them. Taking out an empty shell of a small horseshoe crab I have in my collection of seashore objects, I held it up to the light. Immediately I could see light coming through the transparent eyespots in the carapace. Two very small simple eyes were at the base of the forward spine, and two larger compound eyes bulge from the base of spines on each side of the carapace.

By experimenting with living crabs, scientists have discovered that the animal reacts to polarized light. Its eyes detect the light, although they do not see objects. It is believed that the eye tissues constitute a polarized light compass that guides the crab (also the honey bee) as it navigates from place to place. The image of the distant light source is fixed on a specific point in the retina of the eye and acts as a compass point.

The eyes on the crustaceans, such as the crayfish, crab, and lobster, are more obvious. They are mounted conspicuously at the end of movable stalks, which are on either side of the head. Another interesting example in this group is the freshwater crustacean called cyclops. It is one of the rare animals with a single compound eye instead of a pair.

Other curious photoreceptors found among invertebrate animals are the open pitlike visual organs of the limpet and the pinhole eyes of the

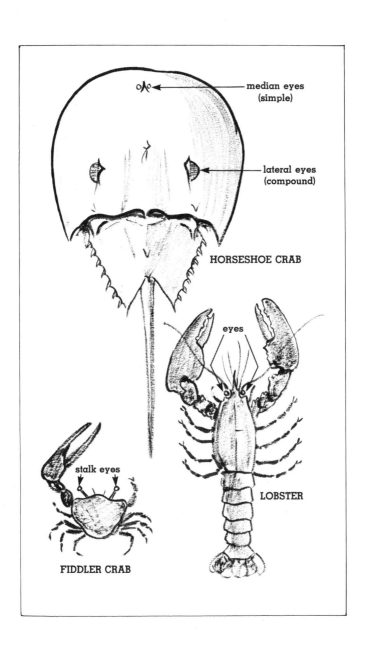

median eyes
(simple)

lateral eyes
(compound)

HORSESHOE CRAB

eyes

LOBSTER

stalk eyes

FIDDLER CRAB

chambered nautilus. The squid and the octopus, on the other hand, have eyes that closely resemble the vertebrate eyes and that also form images.

What might happen to animal life if the world should suddenly be plunged into total darkness and stayed that way permanently? Some animals that now live in lightless environments might continue to exist for a short time, but all life would end without sunlight. The sun's warmth and energy made life on earth possible, and its influence on the evolution of animal life brought about the development of organs that perceive light. Some of these organs are mere cells that see light only faintly, while others are marvelous visual mechanisms that enable animals to see colors and objects clearly.

Some eyes serve to warn an animal of danger; some are like built-in compasses that enable an animal to direct its movements. Photosensory cells in the skin detect bright light, and compound eyes see thousands of images coming from different directions all at once. There are eyes that see in the dark or underwater; some are far-sighted, others nearsighted. All animals do not see equally well, but most of them are dependent upon or influenced by the vibrations of light that originate from the sun.

INDEX

*Indicates illustrations

George F. Mason spent his boyhood on a New England farm outside of Worcester, Massachusetts. After graduating from art school, he worked for two years on a newspaper as a political cartoonist. This, however, did not satisfy his ambition to draw and study animals, so, at the suggestion of Charles Livingston Bull, the famous illustrator of animals, Mr. Mason went to New York City, where he joined the staff of the American Museum of Natural History. During his first ten years there, Mr. Mason helped create the Museum's splendid permanent exhibits in the North American Hall. His special interest has been Alaska and he has traveled there extensively, including three expeditions for the Museum, to study the various wild animals in their native habitats. Later Mr. Mason became Assistant Curator of the Department of Education in the Museum. He now lives in Princeton, Massachusetts.